MARSHES AND SWAMPS

A Wetland Web of Life

Philip Johansson

Enslow Elementary

an imprint of

Enslow Publishers, Inc.

40 Industrial Road
Box 398
Berkeley Heights, NJ 07922
USA

http://www.enslow.com

Library of Congress Cataloging-in-Publication Data

Johansson, Philip.
    Marshes and swamps : a wetland web of life / Philip Johansson.
        p. cm. — (Wonderful water biomes)
    Includes bibliographical references and index.
    ISBN-13: 978-0-7660-2814-2
    ISBN-10: 0-7660-2814-3
    1. Marsh ecology—Juvenile literature. 2. Swamp ecology—Juvenile literature. I. Title.
    QH541.5.M3J63 2007
    577.68—dc22

                                                    2006039769

Printed in the United States of America

10 9 8 7 6 5 4 3 2 1

To Our Readers: We have done our best to make sure all Internet Addresses in this book were active and appropriate when we went to press. However, the author and the publisher have no control over and assume no liability for the material available on those Internet sites or on other Web sites they may link to. Any comments or suggestions can be sent by e-mail to comments@enslow.com or to the address on the back cover.

Every effort has been made to locate all copyright holders of material used in this book. If any errors or omissions have occurred, corrections will be made in future editions of this book.

Illustration Credits: Copyright © 1987, 1998 by Dover Publications, Inc.

Photo Credits: Dr. Ed Standora, pp. 7, 8; Dr. Harold Avery, p. 6; © Ingrid Visser/Foto Natura/Minden Pictures, p. 23 (crab); James Gathany/Wikipedia, p. 28, 40; © 2007 Jupiterimages Corporation, pp. 17, 21, 36, 39; Photo Researchers, Inc.: Andrew J. Martinez, pp. 20 (striped bass), 23 (striped bass), Anthony Mercieca, pp. 20 (muskrat), 23 (muskrat), 41, Dan Suzio, p. 32, F. Stuart Westmorland, pp. 31, 34, 37 (right); Francois Gohier, pp. 11, 18, Gregory G. Dimijian, M.D., p. 12, Harry Rogers, p. 23 (spider), John Kaprielian, pp. 20 (fiddler crab), 22, Martin Dohrn, p. 37 (left), Michael P. Gadomski, pp. 14–15, 16, 26, 33, Millard H. Sharp, pp. 44, 45, Robert Isear, p. 23 (marsh grass), St. Meyers, pp. 20 (sedge plant), 27, Terry Whittaker, p. 29, Vladimir Ivanov, p. 30; Richard King, p. 5; © Robert DeGoursey/Visuals Unlimited, p. 23 (clamworm); Shutterstock, p. 43; © Stephen Dalton/Minden Pictures, p. 42; © Wil Meinderts/Foto Natura/Minden Pictures, pp. 23 (mussel), 38.

Cover Photos: Shutterstock; Michael P. Gadomski/Photo Researchers, Inc. (lower left).

Back Cover: Michael P. Gadomski/Photo Researchers, Inc.

Dr. Hal Avery is a herpetologist at Drexel University who studies the biology of diamondback terrapins at Barnegat Bay, New Jersey. The volunteers depicted in Chapter 1 are from Earthwatch Institute, a nonprofit organization. Earthwatch supports field science and conservation through the participation of the public. See **www.earthwatch.org** for more information.

Table of
CONTENTS

CHAPTER 1
Beneath the Surface 4

CHAPTER 2
The Wetland Biome 10

CHAPTER 3
Biome Communities 19

CHAPTER 4
Wetland Plants 25

CHAPTER 5
Wetland Animals 35

Words to Know 46

Learn More 47
(Books and Internet Addresses)

Index 48

BENEATH *the* SURFACE

Dr. Hal Avery cuts off his boat's motor. He glides to a stop near a low island on the New Jersey coast. Marsh grass grows thick all around him. It waves in the soft, salty breeze blowing from the nearby shore. In the distance, dark pine trees stand on higher ground, the only thing visible above the flat green marsh.

One of the volunteers reaches over the side of the boat to pull a hoop trap from the shallow water. The trap is made of a net on metal hoops. Pieces of crab inside the net are the bait. Today the trap also holds one of the most beautiful residents of the salt marsh. It's what the research team was hoping for: a diamondback terrapin. The turtle is the size of an apple pie. It has brilliant yellow-and-white patterns on its skin and deep grooves in the plates of its shell.

Diamondback terrapins are an important part of the salt marshes along the Atlantic shore of the United States. They nest on the banks of creeks and

Diamondback terrapins live in the salt marsh. Dr. Avery and his team study these turtles in New Jersey.

small islands, and hunt for food under the water. Terrapins are just one of the animal groups that makes the marsh its home.

Turning Up Turtles

"This one is a female, you can tell just from the size of it," says Avery, cradling the animal carefully in his hands. He turns it over and looks at the bright yellow underside of the turtle's shell. "Males are just half this size."

Dr. Avery's assistants use a hoop trap to capture terrapins.

The team works quickly so that they can return the terrapin to the water. The two volunteers take measurements of the turtle's shell. Then they weigh the animal with a hanging scale, dangling her over the boat in a mesh bag. They use other instruments to take measurements of the water: its temperature, how salty it is, how

murky it is. One of them uses a Global Positioning System (GPS) unit to document exactly where they are, while the other takes notes.

This terrapin's shell is being measured.

Avery shows the volunteers how to give the animal a unique mark. He files notches in the edges of her shell. He also injects a tiny microchip, the size of a grain of rice, just under her skin. If they find this turtle again, they will be able to use a scanner to detect this "tag."

"Now we will always know this individual," says Avery. "We hope that next time we find her, she has

a nest. Then we can mark all of her hatchlings as well." He carefully lowers the turtle into the water and releases her. She swims quickly into deeper water and disappears among the marsh plants.

The Wet Lands

Salt marshes like the one where Dr. Avery works are one kind of wetland. A wetland is an area of land covered with shallow water. It is part land, part water. Salt marshes are found by the ocean. Their water is salty and comes and goes with the tide. Marshes and swamps that are farther away from the coast are covered with freshwater.

Diamondback terrapins live in salt marshes from Massachusetts to Texas. They are the only turtle found in these waters, and they face many threats. In the early 1900s, terrapins were a favorite gourmet

food item, so they were hunted in great numbers. Now they are often accidentally drowned in crab traps or killed by boat propellers. By studying the lives of diamondback terrapins, Dr. Avery is learning how to protect these special turtles and their salt marsh home.

WHAT IS A BIOME?

Marshes, swamps, and other wetlands are one kind of biome. A biome is a large area of the earth where certain plants and animals live. They survive there because they are well suited to the environment found in that area.

Each biome has plants that may not be found in other biomes. Soil, water, rocks, and climate all help to determine the kinds of plants that grow there. Marsh grass grows in marshes but not in forests. Cacti grow in deserts but not in the tundra. The animals that eat these plants help form the living communities of a biome. Learning about biomes is a good way to start understanding these plant and animal communities.

Chapter 2

The WETLAND BIOME

Marshes, swamps,

and other wetlands can be found all around the
world. There are wetlands in Arctic Canada and
wetlands in tropical Brazil. They range in size from
less than an acre to hundreds of square miles.
Wetlands are often on the edges of rivers,
lakes, or oceans,
where the water meets
the land. They can also be

found away from these other bodies of water, where dips in the land capture rainwater or water that seeps up from underground.

The one thing all wetlands have in common is that they are covered with water for at least part of the year. The water is shallow, usually not more than a few feet deep. Some wetlands, like riverside swamps, are watery all the time. Others, like salt marshes, may be wet or dry depending on the daily tide. Some wetlands may even be dry for most of

The Florida Everglades are flooded grasslands that cover hundreds of square miles.

the year, when they will look much like grasslands or forests. For at least part of the year, however, they are flooded.

Airless Soil

The soil in marshes, swamps, and other wetlands is different from other soils. It is usually waterlogged. Only certain kinds of plants, such as salt marsh cordgrass and cypress trees, can grow in wetland soil.

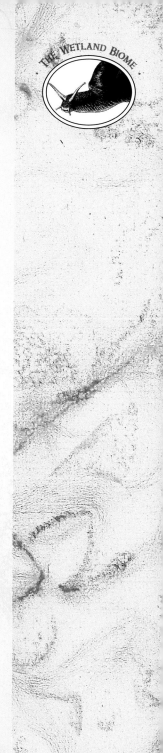

The lack of air also affects wetland plants after they die. They sink to the bottom of the water. Dead plants usually need oxygen to decay (break down). Without air, dead plant matter builds up faster than it can decay. The slow decay of plants without oxygen makes a gas that smells like rotten eggs. All that plant matter makes the soil very rich in nutrients—chemicals needed for life.

Kinds of Wet

Freshwater marshes are the most common kind of wetland. They can be recognized by the grasses, reeds, and other plants that grow there. The water level varies from a few inches to a few feet deep. Most freshwater marshes are found near other bodies of freshwater, such as streams, rivers, ponds, and lakes.

Salt marshes have grasses and reeds like freshwater marshes. But they are found near the ocean instead. They provide a place for many fish

A freshwater marsh contains grasses and reeds. Freshwater marshes are the most common type of wetland.

Salt marshes are found near the ocean. The water level in these marshes rises and falls with the tide.

and shellfish to live during some part of their life cycles. High and low tides make the water level in salt marshes rise and fall each day.

Swamps are areas that are often flooded with water, but shrubs and trees can grow there. Like freshwater marshes, swamps usually occur along the edges of rivers and lakes. There are many different kinds of swamps, named for the different trees or shrubs that grow in them. Red maple swamps are found in the northeast United States, cypress swamps in the southeast, and willow swamps in the west. Mangrove forests are saltwater swamps that grow near the ocean. They cover large areas along tropical coastlines around the world.

Cypress swamps are found in the southeastern United States.

✓ **All around:** Wetlands are found throughout the world, wherever water meets land.

✓ **Covered:** Wetlands are covered with water, from a few inches to a few feet, for at least part of the year.

✓ **Soggy soil:** Wetland soil is waterlogged, and therefore low in oxygen. Dead plant matter builds up because it decays slowly in these conditions.

WETLAND FACTS

✓ **Salt or no salt:** Wetlands can be salty, like salt marshes and mangrove swamps, or freshwater, like freshwater marshes or cypress swamps.

✓ **Trees or no trees:** Marshes have grasses, reeds, and other low-growing plants. Swamps usually have trees and shrubs.

BIOME COMMUNITIES

Like biomes

on land, wetlands contain
communities of plants and
animals. Communities are the
groups of living things found
together in a place. Each
living thing has a role in the
community. Some plants and
animals depend on others.

❖ **19** ❖

SUNLIGHT

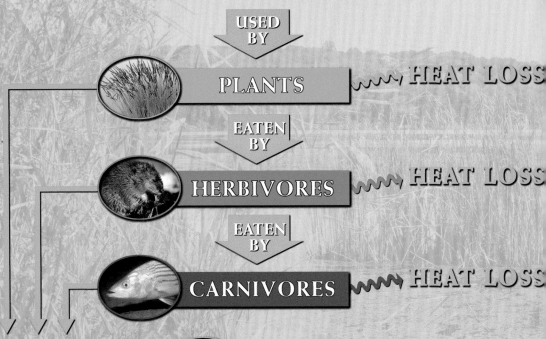

USED BY

PLANTS ~~~ HEAT LOSS

EATEN BY

HERBIVORES ~~~ HEAT LOSS

EATEN BY

CARNIVORES ~~~ HEAT LOSS

DETRITIVORES

eat dead plants and animals

Energy Flow in a Wetland

Salt marsh plants, such as cordgrass or eelgrass, trap the sun's energy for their food. They use the sun's energy to make sugars from carbon dioxide (a gas in the air and dissolved in the water). They store the sugars and use the energy later to live and to grow.

Some animals, such as insects called plant hoppers and snails called periwinkles, have to eat plants to get their energy. Animals that eat only plants are called herbivores. Other animals eat animals. They are called carnivores. Herons, gulls, and diamondback terrapins are carnivores. Some animals, such as raccoons, eat both plants and animals. They are called omnivores.

Other animals get their energy from plants and animals after they die. They break down the dead plant and animal matter in wetland soils. This matter is called detritus. The animals are called detritivores. They capture nutrients from the detritus. Then they return these nutrients to the wetland system. Crabs, sandworms, and other detritivores do this job.

The great blue heron is a carnivore. It gets its energy from eating other animals.

The Food Web

Acre for acre, salt marshes are among the most productive areas on earth. This means they

produce more plant matter in a year than most other grasslands or forests. They even make more plant matter than tropical rain forests. All those plants can then feed and make homes for lots of animals. An acre of salt marsh can produce up to ten tons of plants and animals each year.

The flow of energy through the wetland from the sun to plants to herbivores to carnivores and detritivores follows a pattern called a food web.

SOME PLANTS AND ANIMALS IN THE
SALT MARSH FOOD WEB

PLANTS

Eaten by →

Cordgrass

Sedges

Grasses

Eelgrass

Green algae

Plankton plants

HERBIVORES

Eaten by →

Plant hoppers

Muskrats

Voles

Periwinkles

Crabs

Plankton animals

CARNIVORES

Spiders

Dragonflies
Minnows
Terrapins

Striped
Bass

Egrets
Herons
Eagles
Clams

Mussels

Shrimp

DETRITIVORES

Copepods   Snails   Fungi
Nematodes   Bacteria Crabs

Like a spider's web, it is a complicated network of who eats what or whom. The web connects all the plants and animals of a wetland community. For instance, tadpoles eat algae. Herons, in turn, eat tadpoles. When a heron dies, crabs help break down its body.

Together, plants and animals pass energy through the wetland community. They also use some of the energy to live. At each stage of the food web, some energy is lost as the animals use it. It is lost in the form of heat. More energy from the sun has to be trapped by plants to keep the community alive.

By looking at the plants and animals of the wetland biome, you will see how they may rely on each other. If you take any plant or animal away, it could change how the community works.

WETLAND PLANTS

You need

a boat to explore most
wetlands, but they are well
worth the visit. Salt marsh
grasses wave like flags in
the wind. Cypress trees arch
overhead like a green cathedral.
An even closer look can reveal
what makes these plants so special.

The cattail
uses its stem
to carry air
down to
its roots.

Although all plants need water, most plants would die in a wetland because there is just too *much* water. Plants need oxygen from the air to survive. Most plants get this air from the soil, through their roots. Wetland plants grow in soil that is full of water, which allows very little air to reach their roots.

Some wetland plants, such as cattails, have a stem that is hollow like a straw. The stem can carry air down to the roots so that the plant can breathe and grow.

The lack of air in wetland soils can also make it hard for seeds to grow. Many wetland plants make more plants without using seeds. Some send out underground shoots called rhizomes. The rhizomes grow a new plant that is connected to the same root system as the

Wetland plants, like these sedges, make more plants without using seeds. Instead, special roots called rhizomes grow underground. Then a new clump of the same plant can grow.

first one. This way, a thick group of wetland plants can grow from one individual.

Living With Salt

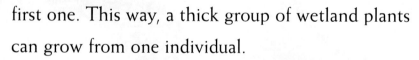

Plants that live in wetlands near the ocean have to deal with more than just flooded soil. They have to live with salt water, which is harmful to most plants. Salt marsh cordgrass grows in dense groups as tall as six feet. It actually soaks up salt and then lets it ooze out through tiny holes in its leaves.

MARSHES AND SWAMPS

Salt marsh plants soak up salt from the water in which they grow. This mangrove leaf gets rid of salt by releasing it through its openings.

If you look closely, you can see salt crystals on the blades of cordgrass.

Beneath the water, other kinds of plants grow. For example, eelgrass is a plant with ribbonlike leaves that covers large areas of the muddy bottom. Green algae are leafy green seaweeds that wave in shallow water.

Mangrove forests are filled with small mangrove trees. They grow in tropical coastal wetlands, such as on the coast of Thailand. Mangrove trees stand up on stiltlike roots, which support their weight in the mucky soil. They have small openings on their roots and stems that allow air in. Their seedlings develop in the tops of the trees and drop only when they are big enough to survive in the flooded soil.

Keeping It Fresh

Freshwater wetlands also have water-logged soils, but without the salt.

stiltlike roots

These wetlands tend to have more kinds of plants growing in them. Freshwater marsh plants come in many forms and grow in different depths of water. Because they are so different and do not need the same food and growing conditions, many kinds of plants can live near each other.

Mangrove trees breathe through pores in their roots. Their stiltlike roots hold them up.

Some plants grow in very shallow water, usually near the edge of the wetland. They are rooted underwater but stand up out of the water. These include many familiar plants, like cattails, as well as others such as rushes, reeds, and sedges. Pickerelweed has heart-shaped leaves with spikes of purple flowers, and arrowhead has arrow-shaped leaves.

Pickerelweed (left) grows in the shallow waters of freshwater wetlands.

Floating plants grow in slightly deeper water. Rather than sticking up out of the water, their leaves float on the water's surface. Most of them are rooted in the mud below. Pondweeds and water lilies have showy floating flowers. Others, like duckweed, have no roots. Masses of tiny, round duckweed plants form a layer that can cover the water's surface.

Water lilies (above) have leaves that float on top of the water.

A third group of freshwater wetland plants are harder to find. They grow completely beneath the surface of the water. Some are rooted in the soil,

while others are not. Wild celery, a plant with long, slender leaves, has roots. Coontail, a plant with leaves like a bushy tail, floats freely below the surface. Many kinds of tiny algae also grow on the surface of rocks and plants or float in the water.

Duckweed has no roots and floats on the surface of the water. It can cover the water's surface like a blanket.

Standing Tall

Trees and shrubs that can live in waterlogged soils grow in swamps. They often have bulges at the base of the trunk (below the water but above the mud). These wide trunk areas help hold up the tree in the wet, mucky soil. Some trees, such as cypress, also develop "knees," parts of the root system that rise above the water surface. The reason for knees is unknown.

They may help support the tree or provide additional oxygen to the roots. Other trees and shrubs that grow in swamps include red maple, white cedar, alder, buttonbush, and willow.

Whether tidal or freshwater, marsh or swamp, the world's wetlands are full of plant life. These plants, in turn, are the source of nutrients and shelter for wetland animals.

Willow trees that grow in swamps do not grow tall because the soft mud cannot support big trees.

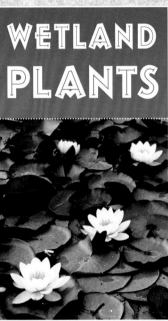

WETLAND PLANTS

✓ **Sucking air:** Because wetland soils are full of water and low in oxygen, wetland plants have special features that allow them to bring air down to the roots.

✓ **Clone rangers:** Many wetland plants reproduce by sending out rhizomes, under-ground shoots from which new plants grow.

✓ **Sweating salt:** Cordgrass and some kinds of mangroves deal with living in salt water by secreting salt from tiny holes in their leaves.

✓ **Wet diversity:** Marshes have many different kinds of plant forms, including plants that stick out of the water, floating plants, and plants beneath the water.

✓ **Wet trees:** Swamp-growing trees have special features that allow them to grow in waterlogged soil, including bulges at the base.

WETLAND ANIMALS

Because wetlands are the border between dry land and open water, you can find animals from both wet and dry habitats there. Many animals come to these wetlands from nearby areas for part of their life cycle. Everything from tiny insects to huge moose can be found visiting wetlands. They may come to feed, to have babies, or just to hide from predators among the dense plants.

❖ **35** ❖

Animal Visitors

Frogs, toads, and salamanders lay their eggs in the water of wetlands. Some of these amphibians spend their adult lives on the land. However, they must return to the water each spring. Their young grow in the water before stepping onto land for the first time. Some insects, like dragonflies and mosquitoes, are familiar on land, but they spend the first stage of their lives in wetlands.

Frogs live in the water and on land. They lay eggs in the water. The tadpoles that hatch stay in the water until they grow legs.

Sandpipers and plovers are types of shorebirds. They and other shorebirds fly thousands of miles every year to nest in wetlands in the Arctic. Other birds, such as geese and ducks, also follow chains of wetlands as they migrate in the spring and fall. Many young fish, such as striped bass, spend time feeding and growing

in wetlands. They move into deeper water as adults. In fact, many animals could not live without wetlands.

Because wetlands are less common than they once were, some wetland animals have become extinct or are in danger of disappearing. For example, tiger salamanders rely on wetlands that are growing scarce in California. More than 40 percent of the species listed as endangered in the United States depend on wetlands for some stage of their lives. These include wood storks and American crocodiles.

Mosquitoes (top, left) spend the early part of their lives in the water of wetlands.

Sandpipers (above, right) travel to wetlands to nest.

Saltwater Animals

Mussels can be found at the surface of the soil where there are lots of plankton for them to eat.

Some of the plants and animals in the salt marsh food web live above the water. Periwinkle snails move up and down the stalks of cordgrass and rushes. They graze on the algae growing there. Plant hoppers suck the juices from salt marsh plants. Spiders, dragonflies, and birds in turn feed on these insects. Even with all this activity, only a small fraction of the action in the salt marsh happens where you can easily see it. The rest of it takes place below the water line.

The deep layers of decaying plants in salt marshes provide lots of food for a variety of animals. Countless tiny living things—invisible to the naked eye—feast on the dead plants. They include bacteria, fungi, nematode worms, and little animals related to shrimps and lobsters called copepods. Many animals that come out

of the water, like insects, crabs, and snails, also look for food in the muck. Clams buried in the soil and mussels anchored to the soil surface filter tiny plankton from the water.

Some fish, like silversides, killifish, and minnows, spend their lives in salt marshes eating copepods and worms. Larger fish, like striped bass, swim through the channels of salt marshes at high tide looking for these fish or unsuspecting crabs. Diamondback terrapins hunt for smaller insects, snails, fish, and worms among the marsh plants.

This African fish eagle spots its prey from above, then dives down to the water and grabs it with the talons on its feet.

At low tide, wading birds eat their share of fish, crabs, and clams. At high tide, ospreys and eagles will swoop down on the marsh for a meal of fish.

Freshwater Animals

Freshwater marshes have many kinds of plants to eat, so more herbivores live there than in salt marshes. Above the water, grasshoppers, caterpillars, and other plant-eating insects live well. Thousands of mosquitoes and flies lay their eggs in the still water. The eggs develop into wormlike larvae that

Mosquitoes lay their eggs in the marsh water. When they hatch, the larvae float just under the surface. They eat aquatic plants.

float just below the surface, sucking the juice out of
aquatic plants. Tadpoles, minnows, and crayfish—
small lobsterlike animals—move along the bottom
in search of algae.

Ducks and geese eat duckweed, algae, and duck
potatoes. These are the fleshy roots of the arrowhead
plant. Muskrats and voles feed on grass, and beavers

Muskrats feed on the grass found in wetlands.

Diving beetles prey on insects below the water's surface.

chew the bark off sticks they drag into the water. Deer browse on buds and branches of willows and other woody plants along the edge of the water. All the animals move aside when a moose wades into the water to eat aquatic plants.

Many predators find their dinner in freshwater wetlands. Dragonflies, spiders, and giant diving beetles eat the many insects that hover over, or swim below, the water's surface. Deerflies, blackflies, mosquitoes, and no-see-ums feast on the blood of mammals. While tadpoles eat algae, grown frogs and toads eat insects. Fish, such as bluegill sunfish, eat mosquito larvae and other aquatic insects.

Many wetland animals hunt other animals. Red-winged blackbirds, yellow-headed blackbirds, and marsh sparrows have nests near the wetland. They feed on the banquet of insects. Long-legged birds,

such as herons, rails, and bitterns, hunt for fish and amphibians. River otters and minks, with their sleek bodies and thick coats, are ideally suited for hunting in the wetland for fish and crayfish. Even foxes and raccoons visit wetlands in search of small prey. Through these many hunters, the energy and nutrients in the wetland get recycled again and again.

Yellow-headed blackbirds build their nests near wetlands. They use the insects that live there to feed themselves and their young.

Raccoons visit wetlands in search of food.

Whether freshwater or salt water, the world's wetlands are important habitats for a wide variety of plants and animals. Many animals could not survive without wetlands being available for part of their life cycle. Scientists like Dr. Hal Avery are learning more about how wetlands work, and how the plants and animals that live there rely on one another. With this information, people can do a better job of managing wetlands to provide for plants and animals in the future.

The biome between: Animals from neighboring land and water habitats often use wetlands at some stage in their life.

Eating decay: Fiddler crabs and blue crabs are among the many animals that eat decaying plant matter, an important job in the salt marsh food web.

Cycle of life: Salt marsh animals time their activity with the tides. Snails and mussels

WETLAND ANIMALS

are active during high tide. Egrets and other predators hunt at low tide.

Swimming insects: Mosquitoes and dragonflies lay their eggs in wetlands; the young hatch and the larvae develop underwater.

From herbivore to carnivore: While tadpoles eat algae beneath the water's surface, grown frogs eat insects from the air.

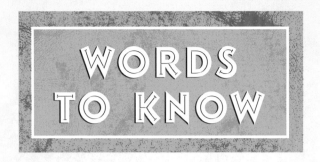

WORDS TO KNOW

bacteria—Tiny living things made of one simple cell.

biome—An area defined by the kinds of plants and animals that live there.

carnivore—An animal that eats other animals.

climate—The long-term pattern of temperature and rain- and snowfall for a given area.

community—All the plants and animals living in any area.

detritivore—An animal that eats dead plant and animal matter (detritus).

detritus—Loose pieces of decomposing plant and animal matter.

food web—The transfer of energy from the sun to plants to herbivores to carnivores and to detritivores.

fungi—Plantlike living things that live on decaying plant matter.

habitat—The area in which a certain plant or animal normally lives, eats, and finds shelter.

herbivore—An animal that eats plants.

marsh—A wetland dominated by grasses, reeds, and other low plants.

nematodes—Tiny round worms that live in the mud.

nutrients—Chemicals necessary for plants and animals to live.

omnivore—An animal that eats both plants and animals.

plankton—Tiny plants and animals that float in the water.

swamp—A wetland that includes shrubs and trees.

tides—The rising and falling of the ocean water level in response to the pull of the moon and sun.

BOOKS

Johnson, Rebecca L. *A Journey Into a Wetland.* Minneapolis: Carolrhoda Books, 2004.

Lawlor, Elizabeth. *Discover Nature in Water and Wetlands: Things to Know and Things to Do.* Mechanicsburg, Penn.: Stackpole Books, 2000.

Stewart, Melissa. *Life in a Wetland.* Minneapolis: Lerner Publications, 2003.

Wallace, Marianne D. *America's Wetlands: Guide to Plants and Animals.* Golden, Colo.: Fulcrum Publishing, 2004.

INTERNET ADDRESSES

Gale Schools. *Wetland Biomes.*
http://www.galeschools.com/environment/biomes/wetland/index.htm

University of California Museum of Paleontology. *Wetlands Gallery.*
http://www.ucmp.berkeley.edu/glossary/gloss5/biome/wetlands/wetlandsgallery.htm

U.S. Environmental Protection Agency. *Wetlands.*
http://www.epa.gov/owow/wetlands/

INDEX

A
air, 13, 26, 28
algae, 24, 28, 32, 38, 41, 42
amphibians, 36, 43
Avery, Hal, 4, 6–9, 44

B
bacteria, 38
beavers, 41
biomes, 9

C
carbon dioxide, 20
carnivores, 21, 22
cattails, 26, 31
communities, 9, 19
cordgrass, 12, 20, 27, 28, 38
cypress trees, 12, 16, 25, 32

D
decay, 13, 38
detritivores, 21, 22
diamondback terrapin, 5,
    8–9, 21, 39

E
eagle, 40
eelgrass, 20, 28
extinction, 37

F
food web, 21–22, 24, 38
freshwater marsh, 8, 13, 16,
    29, 31, 33, 40, 42, 44
fungi, 38

G
Global Positioning System
    (GPS), 7
grasses, 13, 25

H
habitats, 35, 44
herbivores, 21, 22, 40

I
insects, 21, 35, 36, 38, 39,
    40, 42

L
lakes, 10, 13, 16
larvae, 40, 42

M
mangrove forests, 16, 28
microchip, 7

N
nutrients, 13, 21, 33, 43

O
omnivores, 21
oxygen, 13, 26, 33

P
plankton, 39
plant matter, 13, 22
plants, 8, 9, 12–13, 19,
    20–21, 22, 24, 25–29,
    31–33, 35, 38, 39, 40,
    41–42, 44
plovers, 36

pondweeds, 31

R
red maple, 16, 33
reeds, 13, 31
rhizomes, 26
rivers, 10, 13, 16
roots, 26, 28, 31–33, 41

S
salt crystals, 28
salt marsh, 5, 8, 9, 11, 13,
    16, 21–22, 26–27, 38–40
salt water, 27, 44
seaweeds, 28
sedges, 31
seeds, 26
shelter, 33
shrubs, 16, 32–33
soil, 9, 12–13, 21, 26, 27,
    28, 31, 32, 39
sunlight, 20, 22, 24
swamps, 8, 10, 11, 12, 16,
    32, 33

T
tide, 8, 11, 16, 39–40
trees, 12, 16, 25, 28, 32–33

W
water level, 13, 16
water lilies, 31